DICTION I: THE PARADOX OF FEELING

DICTION I: THE PARADOX OF FEELING

A Dictionary Under Constraint

by J. A. Gucci

TABLE OF CONTENTS

INTRODUCTION

Why Study Feeling Structurally?

Most approaches to feeling begin with experience.

A feeling is named, described, remembered, confessed, interpreted, or expressed. The language moves inward toward personal reflection. Meaning emerges through narrative, metaphor, symbolism, memory, or emotional declaration.

Diction I proceeds differently.

The poems in this volume do not attempt to describe feelings directly. Instead, they place named emotional states in correspondence with observable systems drawn from the physical world.

A glacier fractures.

A river jams against itself.

A bell absorbs a strike.

A moth circles a floodlight.

A lake becomes isolated from its river.

These phenomena remain what they are. They do not symbolize emotion. They do not disguise human experience. They are presented as observable systems undergoing pressure, transformation, accumulation, release, recursion, fracture, recovery, or persistence.

The question underlying this book is simple:

Can a feeling be approached through structure
rather than description?

The answer proposed here is that many emotional
states share behavioral patterns with observable
systems. Anxiety, isolation, forgiveness, longing,
hope, shame, and remorse often exhibit
recognizable structural characteristics. By studying
those characteristics within physical phenomena,
emotional conditions become available for
observation without requiring confession or
interpretation.

This approach emerges from the framework of
Absolute Composition, a compositional method
grounded in compression, threshold behavior,
structural correspondence, and observable
transformation.

Readers need not be familiar with that framework
to engage with this volume.

Each entry presents:

A feeling.
An observable phenomenon.
A command.

The feeling provides orientation.
The phenomenon provides structure.
The command extracts a behavioral principle from
the system itself.

The purpose is not agreement.

The purpose is observation.

Readers may discover different correspondences
than those presented here. Teachers may adapt the
entries for classroom discussion. Students may
generate new examples. Writers may use the
structures as compositional models.

The poems are intended not only to be read, but
studied.

Nothing here resolves.

It settles.

A NOTE ON READING

Diction I: The Paradox of Feeling is an applied work of *Absolute Composition*. Each entry pairs a named feeling with an observable phenomenon and a behavioral command. The feeling appears as the title. The body of the poem presents a physical system, event, condition, or transformation drawn from the observable world. The command emerges from the behavior of that system.

The poems do not attempt to explain feeling through confession, narrative, symbolism, or metaphor. Instead, they place emotional states in structural correspondence with observable phenomena. The relationship between feeling and phenomenon is not illustrative. It is behavioral.

Readers approaching this volume may find it useful to ask: What is happening? What changes? Where is the threshold? What remains after the transformation? The answers are not hidden. They are structural.

Interpretation remains possible, but structure comes first. Meaning follows arrangement.

Nothing here resolves.

It settles.

*"Nothing here resolves.
It settles."*

SECTION I — FRICTION

15

ALIENATION
/ ˌā-lē-ə-ˈnā-shən/
(noun)

Leaky black
walnut hull

shriveled—
white birch

purple raspberries.

*Command: Breathe only what welcomes you. Learn who
poisons kindly.*

AMBITION
/ am-ˈbi-shən /
(noun)

Fledgling
clutching a dead branch,

raccoon gaze—
chur chur.

Command: Know what watches when you climb.

ANGER
/ˈaŋɡər/
(noun)

Spring river
jagged

jamming the bend
stacked—

splintered timber.

Command: Learn where movement becomes pressure.

ANXIETY
/ˌaŋˈzīətē/
(noun)

Cracked glacier—
sinking floating iceberg.

Command: Let what's hidden rise.

APATHY

/ˈapəthē/

(noun)

Sun-bleached sails on the doldrums.

Command: Move before waiting leaves a mark.

BITTERNESS
/ ˈbi-tər-nəs /
(noun)

Sealed jack pine
cone

blazing
canopy—

pop.

Command: Wait until fire finds you.

COMPLACENCY
/kəm-ˈplā-sᵊn(t)-sē/
(noun)

Dry duff
wet

rotted reeds
alight on the lakebed—

green bloom.

Command: Count what settles.

COMPULSION
/kəm-ˈpəl-shən/
(noun)

Scent of water
dissolved intestines

battering a rock
grey

gasping rot—

glowing orbs:
apricot-red.

Command: Obey what consumes you.

CONFLICT
/ˈkänˌflikt/
(noun)

Dirty snowball nearing the sun—outgassing.

Command: Burn or deflect.

CONFUSION
/kənˈfyüzhən/
(noun)

Fault slip—
wave ricochet—
buoyant mountain roots.

Command: What shifts below may lift without warning.

CRAVING
/ ˈkrā-viŋ /
(noun)

Glimmering bollard,
moonlight on marsh—

a boil birls—
broken bowl.

Command: Crave clearly—or be claimed.

CYNICISM
/ ˈsi-nə-ˌsi-zəm /
(noun)

Beetle bores—

seeping
sap

trap—
litterfall.

Command: Seal it, and let it fester.

DETACHMENT
/di-ˈtach-mənt/
(noun)

Green leaf
stem

corked—

pale
wood-hard veins.

Command: Learn what no longer passes between you.

DISGUST
/di-ˈskəst/
(noun)

A speck of dust
alight—
squirting cucumber.

Command: Touch, and be expelled.

DISMISSIVENESS
/di-ˈmis-iv-nəs/
(noun)

Muddy rain
over desert

varnish—

glimmering
bone-dry.

Command: Let it land, but not enter.

DOUBT
/ˈdaut/
(noun)

A step on grey ice.

Command: Keep your weight where it lands.

DREAD
/ˈdred/
(noun)

Glass lake

plip.

Command: Don't mistake silence for peace.

EMBARRASSMENT
/imˈberəsmənt/
(noun)

Seed over saba,
jar shake—
saba over seed.

Command: Shake it. What's hidden may rise.

ENTITLEMENT
/in-ˈtī-t°l-mənt/
(noun)

Cuckoo's egg
sparrow's nest.

Command: Hatch what you've taken.

ENVY
/ˈen-vē/
(noun)

Pungent green
fuzzy
red-ripe

seedling—
uprooted, rooted

shriveled fruit.

Command: Root where you ruin.

INSECURITY
/ ˌin-si-ˈkyu̇r-ə-tē/
(noun)

Sand sifting
shifting

dune
leaning—

wind waft—
shimmering sea oats.

Command: Watch what holds the holding.

JEALOUSY
/ ˈje-lə-sē /
(noun)

Plate rammed into plate—
summit

rain—
rivers

snow—
glaciers

fireweed—
nestled in a scree slope.

Command: Take, and break.

PANIC
/ ˈpanik/
(noun)

Creeping fault
slippery stone.

Command: Don't trust the stillness.

POSSESSIVENESS
/pə-ˈze-siv-nəs/
(noun)

Anal clasping
over pond

hovering—

Command: Let go, or be taken with it.

RESISTANCE
/ri-ˈzi-stən(t)s/
(noun)

Third—

in a chain of thirds,
second—
not the ninth,
tethered to the first,
beneath the fifth—
a voice in consonance.

Fourth—

once a third,
now second
above the first,
clutching the fifth—
dissonant.

Reeled by root—
yielding—

third,
in a chain of thirds,
a voice in consonance.

Command: Tense, release—again; harmony is born of friction.

SHAME
/ˈshām/
(noun)

A blue octopus
red

shattered
rock—

ink cloud.

Command: Ink hides you; not the break.

SECTION II — FUSION

43

ACCEPTANCE
/ək'septən(t)s/
(noun)

Gale—

leaning willow
calm—

gnarled.

Command: Let the gale teach your shape.

ANTICIPATION
/ an-ˌti-sə-ˈpā-shən /
(noun)

Double slit—
quivering photon.

Command: Draw.

ATTACHMENT
/əˈtachmənt/
(noun)

Limbs raw
rubbing limbs
wet melding limbs

pulsing—
stump.

AWE
/ˈȯ/
(noun)

One thousand atmospheres
slumped on the trench

floor,
flat

fluttering
liquid bodies.

Command: Let immensity revise you.

COMFORT
/ˈkəm-fərt/
(noun)

Warm air
rising

falling,
snow

topped canopy—
nestled

sleepy
vole.

Command: Settle where shelter gathers.

CONFESSION
/kən-ˈfe-shən/
(noun)

Soft wood
rigid wall

smooth,
raindrop—

ripping apart.

Command: Let the drop find the seam.

CONTENTMENT
/ˈkənˈtentmənt/
(noun)

Stirring languid,
still

lump in a mug—
slumped.

Command: Rest where the stillness gathers.

EMPATHY
/ˈempəthē/
(noun)

Bright green
rock rug

neon slug—
splayed under sun.

Command: Learn which changes keep you living.

FORGIVENESS
/ fər-ˈgiv-nəs/
(noun)

Hammer strike—

lead bell—
thud.

Command: Absorb what would echo.

HOPE
/ˈhōp/
(noun)

Whistling wind—
wet flickering wick.

Command: Shield it, but don't smother it.

INTIMACY
/ˈintəməsē/
(noun)

Clung to a vine—
snap—

stink bugs.

Command: Hold fast where falling is shared.

LONGING
/ˈlȯŋ-iŋ/
(noun)

Twilight.

Command: Let it unravel.

LOVE
/ ˈləʊ /
(*noun*)

57

A moon—
falling sideways.

Command: Keep falling together.

PEACE
/sˈpēs/
(noun)

Dropping—
drag,

still fall.

Command: Let the forces balance.

RESPECT
/rɪˈspɛkt/
(noun)

Leafy drifting
crowns,

shimmering shadows
sun-flecked—

ghost pipe.

Command: Grow where the light is given.

SELF
/ˈself/
(noun)

A sand dune
rubbed by an avalanche—

Dorian hum.

Command: Listen to what shapes you.

VULNERABILITY
/ˌvər-nə-ˈbil-ə-tē/
(noun)

Quivering
hand-cradle

himalayan quail
coo—

allopreening.

Command: Tremble openly.

WONDER
/ˈwən-dər/
(noun)

Frozen flat
hovering hexagons—

sun-dogs.

Command: Don't name the second sun.

SECTION III — FRACTURE

CONVERSION
/kənˈvərzhən/
(noun)

Caterpillar soup

twitching
leg—

butterfly.

Command: Yield to the melt.

DENIAL
/diˈnīəl/
(noun)

Cracked mud
lake

slimy
bed burrow

bubble—
air seep.

Command: Breathe what remains.

DESIRE
/ diˈzī(ə)r /
(noun)

Streaking—
moth

moon,
floodlight—

loops.

Command: Notice what turns pursuit into orbit.

DESPAIR
/ diˈsper /
(noun)

Blazing oaks

plumes of white
black

billowing over beach
grey

settled.

Command: See the end before it arrives.

DISAPPOINTMENT
/ ˌdis-ə-ˈpoin(t)-mənt /
(noun)

Green glowing
blue

still
krill

snap jaw—
empty mouth.

Command: Open again.

DISILLUSIONMENT
/ ˌdis-ə-ˈlü-zhən-mənt /
(noun)

Rain seep
drip on lime

stone—
carved into cave

collapse.

Command: Look beneath what appears solid.

FRAGMENTATION
/ ˌfrag-mən-ˈtā-shən/
(noun)

0
1

This—
that.

01

This and—
that:

Awareness.
. . .

01
01

0101

pAtTeRn.
TIME / change.

. . .

01101
01
000
01

Information:
reality.

E. v. o. l. U. T. I. O. N.

. . .

Exchange:
repeat:
exchange:
repeat:

render—
become.

Command: Reassemble until the pieces refuse you.

INDECISION
/ˌin-di-ˈsi-zhən/
(noun)

Snowpack

settled on slope
steep

poised—

Command: Choose before gravity does.

ISOLATION
/ ˌī-sə-ˈlā-shən/
(noun)

River loops
broken necks

covered in silt—
oxbow lake.

Command: Tend the channels between you.

MELANCHOLY
/ˈmelənˌkälē/
(noun)

Flipped

blanket of warm
over cold

air

looming
flat-light

still lake.

Command: Wait for the air to turn.

OBSESSION
/əbˈseshən/
(noun)

Towering brush pile
teetering—

splash!

Command: Stop stacking.

PROCRASTINATION
/ prə-ˌkra-stə-ˈnā-shən/
(noun)

Hare
nestled in snow,

thin shadows,
long—

fox gaze—
snowy toe splay.

Command: Blink.

REMORSE
/ri'mȯrs/
(noun)

A fractured ant hill,
a unified colony.

Command: Let the wound organize you.

REPRESSION
/re-ˈpre-shən/
(noun)

Plugged

cool throat
vibrating hot—

hiss.

Command: Melt what hardened over it.

RESIGNATION
/ˌrezigˈnāshən/
(noun)

Snow capped
jagged

peaks
scraped by wind—

flatlands.

Command: Outlast the shape, not the stone.

SURPRISE
/ sər-ˈprīz /
(noun)

Rain
dry—
lightning

strike!

Command: Watch what reaches the ground.

SECTION IV — FORCE

AUTHORITY
/ ə-ˈthȯ-rə-tē /
(noun)

Sun streaking wind—aurora.

Command: Follow the light to its source.

BALANCE
/ ˈbalən(t)s /
(noun)

Yanked by moon
pulled by sun—

slow steady
wobble.

Command: Keep correcting.

CONSCIOUSNESS
/ˈkän͵shəsnəs/
(noun)

Rumbling—

jasper and chert
tumbling—

spark.

Command: Strike until it lights.

CONTINUITY
/ ˌkäntəˈnüətē /
(noun)

Black billowing plumes
reddish-orange ash

pink whispering bells.

Command: Become the ground for what follows.

CONTRACTION
/kənˈtrakshən/
(noun)

Desert deluge,
dusty hexagons.

Command: Read the shape of what withdrew.

INSPIRATION
/ˌin-spə-ˈrā-shən/
(noun)

Glints and glitter
lake
unfurling

furling
over lake
falling—

petrichor.

Command: Follow what rises.

RESTRAINT
/ ri-ˈstrānt /
(noun)

A block of ice

plucking,
scratching,

polishing,
scraping—

chatter marks.

Command: Leave marks, not scars.

SECTION V — ECHO

93

ADMIRATION
/ ˌad-mə-ˈrā-shən /
(noun)

Still lake—

upright spruce
upside down.

Command: Hold still long enough to see twice.

BELONGING
/bə-ˈlȯŋ-iŋ/
(noun)

Star flickering

embers,
ash—

constellation.

Command: Let the nearer light dim.

CONFIDENCE
/ ˈkänfədən(t)s /
(noun)

Fledgling in a sandbox
pouncing on a stick.

Command: Trust the claw that once only begged.

CURIOSITY
/ ˌkyu̇r-ē-ˈä-sə-tē /
(noun)

Sunbeams in a mouth
dripping—

perfect black body.

Command: Follow what disappears.

DELIGHT
/ də-ˈlīt /
(noun)

Warm air
over cold

an island in the sky.

Command: Follow the horizon upward.

FREEDOM
/ˈfrē-dəm/
(noun)

Hole in the stone wall—
glade.

Command: Look where the wall gives way.

MEMORY
/ˈmemrē/
(noun)

Strata
layered on strata.

Command: Read what's rewritten.

REVERENCE
/ˈrev(ə)rəns/
(noun)

DO . . .
MI . . .

Ah—
two notes.

DO . . .
MI . . .
SOL . . .

Now—
three.

DO . . .
MI . . .
SOL . . .
TE . . .

The grand finale:
four notes.

No extra meaning—
sorry to disappoint.

Eat them.
Chew well.
Flush when done.

Command: Let the meaning arrive without you.

AFTERWORD

Diction I began with a simple question:

Can a feeling be approached through structure
rather than description?

Most writing about emotion begins with
experience. The feeling is named, expressed,
examined, narrated, or interpreted. The language
moves inward toward reflection.

This book proceeds in the opposite direction.

Each entry begins with a feeling but turns
immediately toward the observable world. The
poems do not attempt to explain what a feeling is.
Instead, they present a phenomenon whose
behavior corresponds to the condition named by
the title.

The relationship is structural rather than symbolic.

A glacier fractures.

A bell absorbs a strike.

A moth circles a floodlight.

A cave collapses.

A forest becomes ash and wildflowers.

The phenomena remain themselves. They do not stand in for emotions. They are not allegories. They are not disguises for human experience.

Yet human experience repeatedly appears within them.

This observation became the foundation of the project.

Across disciplines, systems often behave in remarkably similar ways. Ecological systems, geological systems, atmospheric systems, biological systems, social systems, psychological systems, and historical systems all exhibit forms of pressure, threshold, transformation, accumulation, release, recursion, collapse, recovery, and persistence.

The poems in this volume were composed by observing those behaviors and placing them in correspondence with named emotional states.

The resulting work occupies an unusual position. It may be read as poetry. It may also be read as a study of structure, a collection of compositional models, or a set of pedagogical demonstrations.

No single reading is required.

The dictionary form was chosen because dictionaries describe conditions without requiring narrative. They provide names and definitions. This volume preserves that impulse while replacing explanation with observation.

The command attached to each entry serves a related function. Rather than interpreting the phenomenon, it extracts a behavioral principle from it. The command is not a moral lesson. It is an invitation to notice what the system teaches through its own operation.

The hope of this work is not that readers agree with its definitions.

The hope is that they begin looking for their own.

If feeling has structure, then structure can be studied.

If structure can be studied, it can be taught.

And if it can be taught, it can be practiced.

The world remains full of examples.

Nothing here resolves.

It settles.

USING THIS BOOK IN THE CLASSROOM

Each entry may be approached through five structural questions:

1. What observable system is presented?
Identify the physical phenomenon, process, event, or condition described in the poem.

2. Where is the threshold?
Locate the point of transformation, instability, fracture, release, accumulation, or change.

3. What changes?
Describe the movement from one condition to another.

4. Why might this system correspond to the feeling named by the title?
Focus on behavior rather than symbolism. What structural characteristics are shared?

5. What does the command preserve?
Consider how the command emerges from the behavior of the system itself.

Possible classroom activities:

Structural Observation

Read an entry without revealing the title. Ask students to identify the threshold, transformation, and behavioral pattern before introducing the feeling.

Correspondence Analysis

Compare multiple entries and identify recurring structural behaviors such as accumulation, fracture, isolation, release, recursion, containment, or persistence.

Alternative Correspondence

Ask students to locate a different observable system that exhibits similar behavior and write a new entry using the same feeling.

Cross-Domain Transfer

Invite students to identify emotional structures within ecological, geological, biological, social, historical, or technological systems.

Revision Through Compression

Expand an entry into a paragraph, then revise it back into compressed form while preserving the threshold and transformation.

The goal is not interpretive correctness.

The goal is structural awareness.

Meaning may vary.

Behavior remains observable.

STRUCTURAL GLOSSARY

Accumulation
The gradual gathering of pressure, force, material, instability, or potential within a system.

Command
A behavioral principle derived from the observable system presented in the poem.

Compression
The reduction of language to the minimum necessary for preserving structural tension and transformation.

Correspondence
A relationship between systems based on shared behavior rather than symbolic resemblance.

Observable System
A physical phenomenon, event, process, condition, or transformation presented directly within a poem.

Pressure
The force, tension, instability, contradiction, or concentration operating within a system.

Recursion
The return of a condition, behavior, or structure in altered form.

Release
The discharge, resolution, transformation, or redistribution of accumulated pressure.

Structural Correspondence
Behavioral similarity between an emotional state and an observable system.

Threshold
The point or condition at which one state becomes another.

Transformation
A change in condition produced through pressure, duration, accumulation, fracture, release, or interaction.

Persistence
The continuation of a condition after transformation has occurred.

Residue
What remains after a threshold has been crossed.

Behavior
The manner in which a system changes, stabilizes, accumulates pressure, fractures, adapts, recovers, or persists.

Structural Reading
An approach that examines how a system behaves before asking what it means.

COLOPHON

Diction I: The Paradox of Feeling was composed according to the principles of Absolute Composition, a structural framework organized through compression, correspondence, threshold behavior, and observable transformation.

Each entry consists of a feeling, an observable phenomenon, and a command. The poems were constructed through the study of physical, biological, ecological, geological, atmospheric, astronomical, and behavioral systems whose transformations exhibit structural correspondence with the emotional conditions named by their titles.

The collection is organized into five sections:

FRICTION — systems under pressure.

FUSION — systems entering relation.

FRACTURE — systems crossing unstable thresholds.

FORCE — systems shaping and reshaping one another.

ECHO — systems persisting through reflection, residue, memory, and return.

The purpose of the work is neither symbolic substitution nor emotional description. The phenomena remain themselves. Meaning emerges through observable relation and structural arrangement.

This volume serves both as a collection of poems and as an applied study in Absolute Composition.

Composed and structurally refined in the United States.

First Edition, 2026.